Made in United States
Orlando, FL
23 September 2024

51831204R10055